# THE
# OREGON
# TRAIL

by
## LINDA THOMPSON

Rourke
Publishing LLC
Vero Beach, Florida 32964

www.rourkepublishing.com

**PHOTO CREDITS:**
Courtesy Bureau of Land Management: pages 22, 25, 26, 28-29; Dellenbaugh, Frederick S., *Breaking the Wilderness*, 1905: page 11; Courtesy Denver Public Library, Western History Collection, Part of the Alice A. Stewart Hill scrapbook, Call Number X-11929: Cover; Courtesy Fred Hultstrand History in Pictures Collection: page 39; Courtesy of General Libraries, University of Texas at Austin: page 4; Courtesy Library of Congress, Prints and Photographs Division: pages 27, 30, 36, 41; Courtesy L. Tom Perry Special Collections, Harold B. Lee Library, Brigham Young University, Provo, Utah, Item 1072, Item 64, from 18405: pages 20, 23, 36; Courtesy National Parks Service: pages 16, 34, 42; Courtesy Nebraska State Historical Society Photograph Collections: page 41; Courtesy Northwestern University Library, Edward S. Curtis Collection: page 39; Courtesy Rohm Padilla: pages 8, 13; Courtesy Scotts Bluff National Monument: Title Page, pages 6, 7, 12, 14, 15, 17, 19, 20, 31, 33, 37; Courtesy University of Washington Libraries, Special Collections: pages 26, 35.

**SPECIAL NOTE:** Further information about people's names shown in the text in bold can be found on pages 43 and 44. More information about glossary terms in bold in the text can be found on pages 46 and 47.

**DESIGN: ROHM PADILLA**
**LAYOUT/PRODUCTION: ELIZABETH BENDER**

**Library of Congress Cataloging-in-Publication Data**

Thompson, Linda, 1941-
    The Oregon Trail / Linda Thompson.
        p. cm. -- (The expansion of America)
    Includes bibliographical references and index.
    ISBN 1-59515-225-3 (hardcover)
    1. Oregon National Historic Trail--Juvenile literature. I. Title. II.
Series: Thompson, Linda, 1941- Expansion of America.
    F597.T48 2004
    978'.02--dc22

2004010033

**TITLE PAGE IMAGE**
Wagon train heading down the pass

# TABLE OF CONTENTS

Only 20 years after it became independent, the United States gained a region that doubled the country's size. And barely 50 years later, it reached across immense plains and towering mountain ranges to touch the Pacific Ocean. How it grew so fast in such a short time is still an amazing tale. It could never have happened without citizens who were brave and willing to take risks. It also required a government that encouraged people to move into a strange and sometimes frightening new land, 2,000 miles (3,220 km) from any civilization they had known.

Map of the Old Oregon Trail

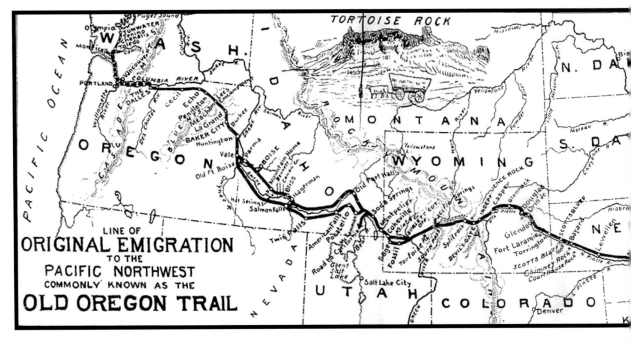

## WHO CLAIMED OREGON?

The first European American to sail into the mouth of the Columbia River was an American seaman, **Robert Gray**, in 1792. His visit gave the United States a claim to Oregon country, but the British claimed Oregon on the basis of their fur-trading activities there. During the **War of 1812**, Britain had gained control of most of the Columbia River. By an 1818 treaty, the U.S. and Britain agreed to jointly occupy the Oregon Territory. Control of Oregon was not finally decided until 1846, when the two countries agreed on the 49th **parallel** as their boundary.

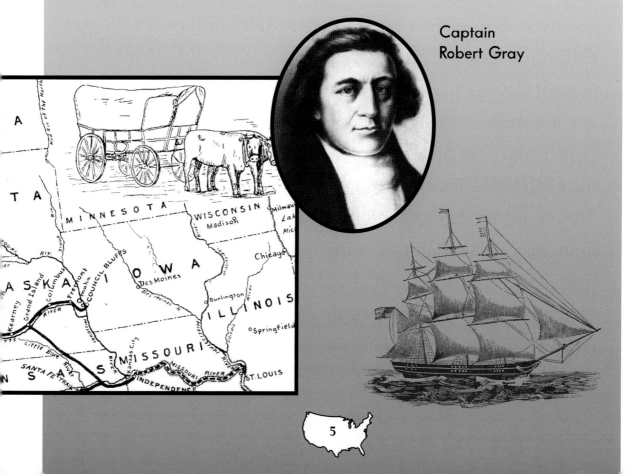

Captain
Robert Gray

Wagons waiting to be ferried across the Missouri River at Council Bluffs, Iowa

More than 300,000 **pioneers** traveled the **Oregon Trail** between 1840 and 1860. They were drawn by the promise of inexpensive or free land where they could grow food, raise livestock, and create a better life for their families. The early **emigrants'** goal was the **fertile** Willamette Valley near present-day Portland, Oregon. After the discovery of gold in California in 1848, many more wagons turned south at Fort Bridger (in present-day southern Wyoming) and took the **California Trail**. They headed for the Sierra Nevada Mountains or the new towns of Sacramento or San Francisco. By 1860, more than 200,000 emigrants had traveled to California and about 53,000 had settled in Oregon. Another 43,000 people used the Oregon Trail to reach Utah, where they founded Salt Lake City. They were **Mormons** who were fleeing religious **persecution**.

The Louisiana Purchase in 1803 set the stage for this immense **migration**. When the year began, the United States had only 17 states and one large **territory.** The country's western border was the Mississippi River. But by the end of 1803, President **Thomas Jefferson** had bought the vast and unknown land called Louisiana from France. Stretching from the Mississippi River to the Rocky Mountains, it included 828,000 square miles (2,144,510 square km) of unknown land. This land was now available for exploration and settlement.

A large train of Mormon handcarts fording a stream in western Wyoming

**OREGON TERRITORY 1846**

**ESTABLISHED 1818**

**CEDED BY MEXICO 1848**

**LOUISIANA PURCHASE 1803**

**GADSDEN PURCHASE 1853**

**TEXAS ANNEXED 1845**

Within half a century, the United States had added the Pacific Northwest through a boundary agreement with England. Texas, a **republic** that had separated from Mexico, joined the United States in 1845. California and the Southwest followed as a result of the Mexican War (1846-1848). By 1853, with the purchase of a strip on the southern edges of Arizona and New Mexico, the **continental** United States (except for Alaska) was complete.

Map of major land additions to the continental United States

**UNITED STATES PRIOR TO 1803**

**CEDED BY SPAIN 1819**

Some adventurous Americans had moved into these regions years before, when they were still claimed by other countries. But the great mass of **immigrants** came to Oregon, California, and Utah after U.S. **acquisition.** By deciding to pack their families and belongings into **covered wagons** and leave home, they began to transform America in a number of ways. One of the most important changes involved the three million Native Americans who lived in the region between the Mississippi River and the Pacific Ocean. Other changes had to do with the growth of cities and states, as well as industries that centered on the rich resources of the West.

By the end of the century, the United States had six times as many people as in 1803, and 25 percent of them lived west of the Mississippi. Within a few **decades**, improvements such as roads, railroads, and the telegraph had made it much easier for those who settled the West to travel, receive mail and supplies, and live comfortably in their adopted homelands.

# Chapter II: TOO WILD AND FAR AWAY

The first people to tread animal paths that became sections of the Oregon Trail were Native Americans. They used the paths to **migrate** between their winter villages and summer hunting grounds, to seek wild plants, and to pursue animals for fur and meat. Natives called the part of the Oregon Trail that crosses the Rocky Mountains the "Big Medicine Trail." Except for a few fur traders, European Americans in the early 19th century stayed east of the Missouri River. Maps showing the territory to the west were extremely inaccurate, based more on imagination than on fact.

Beginning about 1820, **mountain men** began using paths that became parts of the Oregon and California trails. These men made their living by trapping beaver. An English fur-trading business, the Hudson's Bay Company, had operated in western Canada and the Pacific Northwest for several decades. Mountain men such as **Kit Carson, Jim Bridger, Joseph Walker**, and **Jedediah Smith** trapped beaver along streams and rivers, selling pelts to the Hudson's Bay Company and other fur companies.

(Above) Jim Bridger, in his later years. (Below) Kit Carson

## RELUCTANCE TO GO WEST

To most people in the early 19th century, it made no sense to send settlers in large numbers to Oregon territory. It seemed too far from the East and had an "**inhospitable**" climate, according to a New York Congressman. Others mentioned "impenetrable forests... of **prodigious** size" that would block settlement.

Dr. **John Floyd**, a Virginia Congressman and friend of explorer **William Clark**, felt differently. He introduced a bill to make Oregon a territory in 1822, but it failed in the House of Representatives by a vote of 100 to 61.

A fur-trading rendezvous near the Grand Tetons in Wyoming

Many of the pelts were made into beaver hats, a type of hat that was popular in Europe. But when the beaver disappeared after a few years, the mountain men began to work as guides for explorers and eventually for groups of settlers crossing the Rocky Mountains.

Although President Jefferson had sent the **Lewis and Clark Expedition**, or "Corps of Discovery," to explore the Louisiana Purchase in 1804-1806, its findings did not immediately bring about settlement of the Far West. Congressmen and newspaper editors felt that Oregon was too wild and too far away, so additional expeditions were not encouraged.

But a Boston businessman, **Nathaniel Wyeth**, read the journals of Lewis and Clark and decided to take a wagon caravan to Oregon. Wyeth was inspired by the efforts of **Hall Jackson Kelley**, a Massachusetts teacher, who had encouraged settlement of Oregon. Unable to get government support for a wagon train, Kelley traveled there alone. But officials of the Hudson's Bay Company who did not want Americans in what they considered "their backyard" made him feel unwelcome.

A beaver hat that was popular in the 1820s

Wyeth was determined to establish a business in Oregon in fur and fish products. He recruited 24 men in Boston and sent a ship with supplies and seed and farming equipment from Boston. It would sail around the tip of South America and meet Wyeth's party at the mouth of the Columbia River. In St. Louis, Missouri, Wyeth met **William Sublette**, a mountain man who agreed to be his guide. The group rode horses from Independence, Missouri, to the Platte River (in present-day Iowa, Nebraska, and Wyoming). This route became the eastern section of the Oregon Trail. Some of the men turned back, but 11 of them continued on a path somewhat north of the Oregon Trail to the Snake River in present-day Idaho.

The men became lost and nearly starved, but were helped by friendly **Shoshone** Indians. They reached Fort Vancouver (now Vancouver, Washington) on the Columbia River in October, eight months after leaving Boston. Fort Vancouver was the trading post of the Hudson's Bay Company. However, the ship that was supposed to meet them with supplies had been lost at sea. Wyeth was forced to return to Boston. On a second attempt in 1834, he brought 70 men, who blazed a trail along the south side of the Columbia to the site of present-day Portland. This outpost across the river from Fort Vancouver would become Oregon City, the western end of the Oregon Trail.

Shoshone outside of their tipi

On his second expedition, Wyeth built **Fort Hall** near present-day Pocatello, Idaho, to store trading goods that he was unable to sell. Fort Hall became an important stopping place on the trail. When he reached Oregon, Wyeth founded a settlement on an island at the mouth of the Willamette River where it flows into the Columbia near Portland. But his business efforts failed, largely because of resistance from the English traders. In 1836, he sold his interests to the Hudson's Bay Company.

## FORTS

Fort Hall, Fort Laramie, and similar buildings along the trail were not military forts, like Fort Kearny in Nebraska or others, which were built to protect travelers from foreign enemies or Indians. The forts along the Oregon Trail were originally built as trading posts.

Fort Laramie was a popular trading post.

# Chapter III: THE MISSIONARIES AND EARLY FOLLOWERS

One man who came on Nathaniel Wyeth's second expedition, **Jason Lee**, was a **Methodist missionary**.

Cayuse Chief Five Crows

Missionaries were some of the first **migrants** into Oregon country, and they came to convert Native Americans—the **Cayuse**, **Nez Percé**, and other groups of the area—to Christianity. Lee founded a mission at the Dalles, on the Columbia River. In 1836, **Presbyterian** missionaries **Samuel Parker** and **Henry Spalding**, and a physician, Dr. **Marcus Whitman**, followed them. Their wives, **Narcissa Whitman** and **Eliza Spalding**, were the first European-American women to cross the Rockies.

Samuel Parker stayed for two years and then returned to the East Coast. The Whitmans settled near present-day Walla Walla, Washington, and the Spaldings near present-day Lewiston, Idaho.

# THE WHITMAN CARAVAN

Just 10 years before, only the bravest mountain men attempted the Oregon Trail. By contrast, the Whitman expedition included

a group of English sportsmen who had come to hunt buffalo for fun. They had brightly painted wagons, servants, and hunting dogs. The missionary families brought up the rear, carrying far too many belongings. Much of their clothing, boxes of books, and camping gear had to be left along the way.

The mission established by Marcus and Narcissa Whitman

## INDIANS VISIT ST. LOUIS

In 1831, three Nez Percé and one member of the Flathead tribe had visited St. Louis with some traders returning from the West Coast. They came out of curiosity, but an educated member of the **Wyandot** people of Ohio, **William Walker**, heard of their visit and wrote about it to a friend. Walker made up a story about the western Indians traveling to St. Louis to request the "Book of Heaven," or the Bible. A Methodist newspaper published the letter, inspiring missionaries and congregations across the country to answer the call of duty. This letter stirred great interest in the Oregon country among churchgoers and **clergy**.

By this time, the permanent route of the Oregon Trail was well defined. It began at Independence, Missouri, and followed Wyeth's route to the Platte River, 320 miles (515 km) away. Travelers passed landmarks called Courthouse Rock, Scotts Bluff, and Chimney Rock before arriving at **Fort Laramie**, 875 miles (1,408 km) from Independence. This fort was under construction when Wyeth passed through in 1834, and it became a major resting point for pioneers before they headed into the difficult **terrain** of the Rocky Mountain foothills.

After another 280 miles (451 km), wagon trains left the Platte and followed the Sweetwater River to South Pass. A beaver trapper, **Robert Stuart**, had discovered South Pass, guided by

Chimney Rock, in present-day Nebraska

Indians in 1812. Unlike most of the impossibly steep passes through the Rocky Mountains, South Pass was broad and gradually sloping. It was the only place that wagons could cross the Rockies north of New Mexico.

Scotts Bluff, a notable landmark along the Trail

## INDEPENDENCE ROCK

Pioneers looked forward to spotting Independence Rock on the Sweetwater River. About 100 feet (30.5 m) high and one half mile (.8 km) long, it became a monument to those who passed over the Oregon Trail. They could not resist carving their names in the soft limestone for others to see. Most wrote six or eight feet above the ground, but some people climbed higher and marked their names, using knives, tar, gunpowder, and buffalo grease. Many of these names can still be read today on the rock, south of Casper, Wyoming.

(Above) wagons rounding Independence Rock. (Below) signing the rock

Before mountain man Jim Bridger built **Fort Bridger** (1841-1843) as a supply stopover along the trail, pioneers headed west to the Bear River. After 1843, they turned southwest, renewed their supplies at the fort, and continued on their way. Those who were California-bound turned southwest either at Fort Bridger or Fort Hall. They would have to cross another high mountain range, the **Sierra Nevada**. Settlers headed for the Willamette Valley faced Oregon's Blue Mountains and then either the raging waters of the Columbia or a long walk over the Cascade Mountains in late fall. Whether they turned north or south, all travelers risked thirst, hunger, exhaustion, drowning, disease, getting lost, losing pack animals, and freezing to death before reaching their destination.

The Sierra Nevada Mountains were one of a few formidable mountain ranges to cross on the journey west.

The Snake River leads to the Columbia.

On their way to the Columbia, Oregon-bound pioneers trekked 300 miles (483 km) along the Snake River, which wound through a narrow canyon. Before 1843, travelers abandoned their wagons at Fort Hall and continued with pack animals. If the caravan stayed near the river, mosquitoes covered the animals so thickly that at times only their eyes could be seen. If they camped high in the canyon to avoid insects, immigrants faced a dangerous hike down to the river for water. Then, they had to cross the Snake River, always a risky affair. People and animals drowned regularly during the many river crossings they had to make on their 2,000-mile (3,220-km) trip.

The journey was so difficult that Dr. **John McLoughlin**, head of the Hudson's Bay Company at Fort Vancouver, said people might as well plan to go to the moon. **Horace Greeley**, editor of the *New York Daily Tribune*, wrote that it was homicide to send women and children to the West by wagon. He felt the land was too rugged, the route too dangerous, and the U.S. Army could not defend the travelers against either the British or unfriendly Indians.

Horace Greeley

In spite of these warnings, more and more Americans left their homes and headed into the unknown. Often, a man would sell his farm without telling his wife. She was forced to pack up the children, cooking pots, food, and clothing, and go with her husband. The people who left were neither wealthy nor poor. They had to have enough money to make the trip, and selling the farm was often the answer.

An emigrant's grave on the Sweetwater River at Three Crossings, Wyoming

## CAUSES OF DEATH

Drownings were second only to accidental shootings along the Oregon Trail. Men traveled well armed for hunting and to ward off Indian attacks. But not all were used to handling guns. Hundreds of headstones marked graves along the trail, and the notation "Shot himself accidentally" was common. Between 1840 and 1860, more than 300 people drowned while trying to cross rivers. Diseases, especially **cholera**, claimed many lives. The risk of Indian attack was exaggerated—most groups were friendly and helpful—and Indians killed only 362 pioneers between 1840 and 1860. In comparison, travelers killed 426 Natives. All in all, about 10,000 pioneers died along the Oregon Trail in its entire history.

Winchester
rifle

A severe depression in 1837 had made land prices fall on the Missouri **frontier**. Farmers could not sell their produce. To give them a fresh start, Congress passed the **Preemption Act** of 1841, providing that anyone settling on unclaimed land could claim it. The settler had the first right to buy at a guaranteed price, sometimes as low as two dollars an acre (.41 hectare).

Epidemics of disease and unhealthy climates also drove people to go west. The humid valleys of the Mississippi and the Missouri teemed with mosquitoes. In the 19th century, more people died from diseases such as malaria, typhoid, tuberculosis, and scarlet fever than from any other cause. In 1850 alone, about 30,000 Americans died of cholera.

Finally, the institution of slavery contributed to farmers' decisions to head west. Some states allowed slavery, while others did not. Even where slavery was legal, some people found it immoral and refused to own slaves. But farmers and ranchers with slaves had an advantage. They could produce more food, animal hides, cotton, tobacco, or other products and sell them for less because slaves were paid no wages. Rather than try to compete in an unfair situation, some farmers chose to move west and begin from scratch.

Many minorities fled west where they thought there would be less prejudice. This is a re-enactment of traders on the Oregon Trail.

Fort Vancouver, headquarters of the Hudson's Bay Company

By taking wagons to Idaho, Dr. Marcus Whitman had proved that wheeled vehicles could travel the Oregon Trail. The Whitmans wrote many letters home from Walla Walla, praising the Columbia River country and urging that more missionaries be sent. By 1840, about 500 people had followed them to the Willamette Valley.

Covered wagons

In 1840, the **Jesuit** Order sent the first **Catholic** missionary into the Rockies. Father **Pierre Jean De Smet** from Belgium visited Fort Vancouver, but ended up founding his mission among the **Flathead** people in Montana instead.

Migration to California was given a boost by the publication of Richard Henry Dana's book, *Two Years Before the Mast*, in 1840. It described in detail life on the California coast under Mexico in the 1830s. Also, a few California pioneers wrote to East Coast newspapers praising the mild climate and the land. One of California's biggest **boosters** was **John Sutter**, from Switzerland, who had bought a large ranch near the Feather River in the foothills of the Sierra Nevada. He called California "the promised land." Although he had become a Mexican citizen, he began to issue passports and sell land—illegally— to new arrivals. He planned to build a large community and then declare California an independent republic.

Father Pierre Jean De Smet

Re-enactment of a wagon train on the Trail

The first wagon train on the Oregon Trail set out from Independence in 1843. It was bound for California, but 32 of the 66 travelers decided along the way to go to Oregon. By this time, 500 settlers lived on 120 farms in the Willamette Valley with 1,000 Indian servants, 3,000 cattle, and 2,500 horses. Before the Gold Rush of 1849, four or five times as many people chose Oregon over California.

Mountain terrain outside of Salem, Oregon

## MANIFEST DESTINY

In 1845, **John L. O'Sullivan**, the editor of the *New York Morning News*, wrote that it was the United States' "manifest destiny" to spread out and possess the entire continent of North America. He said, "Providence has given [it to] us for the development of the great experiment of liberty and federated self-government entrusted to us." This **doctrine** of Manifest Destiny, combining religious and political motives, looked upon history as having a God-given purpose. It assumed that white people were superior to all others and provided them with a **rationale** for taking over Indian lands. This way of thinking was reflected in the 1844 election of **James K. Polk**, who campaigned on an **expansionist platform**, as president.

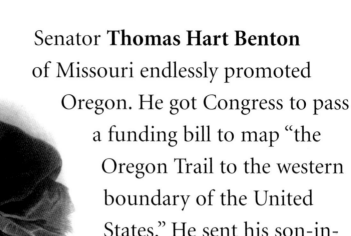

Senator **Thomas Hart Benton** of Missouri endlessly promoted Oregon. He got Congress to pass a funding bill to map "the Oregon Trail to the western boundary of the United States." He sent his son-in-law, **John Frémont**, to map and publicize the trip, with Kit Carson and **Lucien Maxwell** as guides. This expedition left in 1842, taking Benton's 12-year-old son for extra publicity, but when the men learned that attacks by Sioux Indians

Thomas Hart Benton

were likely, they left the boy at Fort Laramie. Frémont turned back at South Pass and the mapping task was abandoned, but his articles about his experience thrilled readers and began to convince them that the Oregon Trail was safe.

Christopher "Kit" Carson

# Chapter IV: THE GREAT MIGRATION

The 1841 and 1842 expeditions set the stage for "the great migration" in 1843. More than 1,000 people with 120 wagons and 5,000 oxen and cattle made up that caravan. In 1843, people were more willing to go because the **economy** had improved. Farmers now had a little money and didn't want to wait for the next **recession**.

When they reached the Platte River, the emigrants began to see buffalo herds numbering in the tens of thousands. Many men were unskilled at hunting them, often using 50 shots on a single animal. If a river had no crossing place, the pilgrims stretched buffalo skins over their wagon beds to dry and then smeared the skins with fat and ashes to make them waterproof. Turned upside down, the wagon was now a makeshift barge. The pioneers reloaded their possessions into them and pulled them across the river with ropes. As many as 50 "barges" might be chained together, pulled by horses or mules from the opposite bank of the river.

Buffalo being hunted with rifles

The travelers in 1843 were surprised when Dr. Marcus Whitman met them on the south bank of the Platte River. He offered to help them get their wagons up the Snake River valley. Despite many difficulties, they were the first pioneers to take wagons so far. When they reached the Columbia River, they built rafts to ferry supplies and animals 100 miles (161 km) to the Dalles. Native guides from the Cayuse, Walla Walla, Spokane, and other tribes helped them **maneuver** their rafts over the swift, dangerous rapids.

## WOMEN ON THE TRAIL

Women in significant numbers began to travel the Oregon Trail in 1842. Rumors of Indian attacks on white women had made them fearful from the start. It was more common, however, for an Indian to admire a woman and offer to buy her. Some women—mostly young unmarried women with some free time—kept diaries. They wrote about the weather, the beauty of nature, difficulties encountered, and their daily chores. For example, we know from Narcissa Whitman's diary that she was able to wash clothes only three times on her eight-month journey. Women had to collect the buffalo dung that was used to fuel fires for cooking. They learned quickly that drinking **alkaline** water made people sick. The saddest diary entries relate to deaths of children, whether from disease or accidents, along the trail.

# WHAT THEY CARRIED

Emigrants saved at least $1,000 per family for the trip. If they had less, they offered to work as cooks, nannies, or wagon drivers. Families carried 200 pounds (91 kg) of flour and 100 pounds (45 kg) of bacon for each member, along with beans, lard, dried fruit, rice, coffee, sugar, salt, and biscuits. They learned to leave behind most heavy items except for shovels and cooking pots. One cookbook from that period indicates that bacon or rice cost 10 cents a pound (.5 kg), coffee 30 cents a pound, dried beans about 3 cents a pound, and sugar about 12 cents a pound. An axe cost $1.25 while a bread pan went for 50 cents. The price of a covered wagon was $100, and oxen were $75 each. The book indicates that supplies for one family's trip to Oregon territory would cost $539.60.

(Right) coffee pot.
(Below) wagon on the
Barlow Toll Road

The last stretch of the Columbia included Cascade Falls. They spent two weeks building a road so they could **portage** around the falls, but many people were ill and exhausted and could go no further. Here Dr. McLoughlin of the Hudson's Bay Company became a savior. Although he had been ordered not to help Americans, he nursed the sick members of the party back to health at Fort Vancouver and gave the pioneers more than $31,000 in emergency money. He also supplied free food, clothing, medicine, tools, seed, cattle, and more to help the settlers get started. On October 27, 1843, the first part of the caravan reached Oregon City and within a few months all 875 settlers had arrived.

The western end of the Oregon Trail is now Ankeny National Wildlife Refuge, Dallas, Oregon.

Columbia River area Natives camp at The Dalles, Oregon.

The success of this caravan caused a sensation back east. "Oregon Fever" took hold, and each year saw more people on the trail. In 1845, 2,500 people went to Oregon and 260 to California. One Oregon immigrant, **Samuel K. Barlow**, proposed building a road over the Cascade Mountains, south of Mount Hood, to bypass the final **perilous** 60 miles (97 km) of the Columbia. In 1846, he returned with a crew of workers and built the road. That year, two-thirds of the pioneers took his cut-off, paying Barlow five dollars a wagon. Barlow was able to repay the construction loan for the road within a year. A section of this road still exists as a U.S. Forest Service Road, and other parts are buried under U.S. Highway 26.

Brigham Young

In 1847-48, Brigham Young led 1,700 Mormons from Illinois to escape religious persecution. They followed the Oregon Trail to a point beyond Fort Bridger, where they turned southwest and followed a cut-off to the Great Salt Lake. Within a few years, thousands more had joined them in their new home, Salt Lake City. They were skilled farmers and quickly grew vegetables and other food products that they could sell. Beginning in 1849, when thousands of gold-seekers poured through, the Mormon pioneers profited by buying unwanted goods at low prices and selling the "**argonauts**" livestock and food at high prices.

Mormon pioneers,
July 1847

The discovery of gold in 1848 at Sutter's Fort in the California foothills changed traffic on the Oregon Trail forever. In 1848, 400 people took the California Trail, but by 1849 there were 25,000 argonauts, and in 1850, 44,000. The trails became huge trash dumps, littered with animal carcasses, bones, wagon parts, and garbage. Also, a new kind of traveler joined the wagon trains from Missouri—the criminal. The desire for gold brought people who would never have attempted the journey drawn only by the promise of land and freedom.

The 1850 national **census** showed that 12,093 people lived in Oregon. Ten years later, 52,495 were counted. One reason for the increase was the Oregon Donation Act of 1850, which gave 320 acres (130 hectares) to a single man or 650 acres (263 hectares) to a married man.

Rutted trail at South Pass, Wyoming

The four-cent Homestead Act stamp was issued in 1962, 100 years after the signing of the act.

In 1862, Congress passed the Homestead Act to encourage young people and laborers in the East to start new lives as independent landowners. The Act granted 160 acres (65 hectares) to anyone who would farm the land. If a settler wished to buy it after living there six months, it cost only $1.25 an acre. By 1890, about two million people had taken advantage of the Homestead Act to create 372,660 farms throughout the West. At the end of the century, 930,000 people lived in the new states of Oregon and Washington.

## THE WHITMAN MASSACRE

In 1847, Dr. Whitman was blamed for a measles epidemic that had killed more than half the tribe of 350 Cayuse. Although the doctor tried to save them, he could not. He was seen as a powerless medicine man who must die, according to their tradition. The Cayuse murdered Marcus and Narcissa Whitman, two children, and 10 other men, taking 47 captives and burning the mission. A pioneer **militia** of 500 men pursued the Cayuse warriors for some two years, eventually capturing and hanging the five who were responsible.

The settlement of Oregon territory and the West had extremely harmful effects on the lives of the three million or so Native Americans living in this region. Thousands of Natives died from European-introduced diseases. Pioneers killed buffalo not just to eat but for sport, and within a few decades, the immense herds were gone. The buffalo were vital to the survival of the **Plains** Indians, supplying them with food, clothing, bedding, hides for homes, and many other necessities. As settlers moved into Native-occupied regions, Natives were forced onto less desirable land or moved to reservations. Natives, especially Plains and **Plateau** groups, rebelled by raiding wagon trains and settlements. Their resistance quickly spelled the end of their freedom, as settlers called for the federal government to do something about "the Indian problem." By 1890, the centuries-old cultures and civilizations of the Native Americans had been largely destroyed.

Lone Chief, a member of the Cheyenne

The completion of a **transcontinental** railroad in 1869 made it faster and easier to move people and freight. Although the railroads were a boon to settlement, they also spelled the end of the great overland trails. Yet the deep ruts from thousands of wagon wheels that had passed over the Oregon Trail marked the routes of future roads and highways.

In 1978, Congress designated the Oregon National Historic Trail, which is managed by the U.S. Forest Service, the Bureau of Land Management, and the National Park Service. State and local governments and private citizens, whose land the trail crosses, also participate. The corridor of the Oregon Trail contains about 300 miles (483 km) of visible ruts and 125 historic sites. An auto route is marked from Independence, Missouri, to Oregon City, Oregon. An "End of the Oregon Trail Interpretive Center" is open to the public in Oregon City, at the southern edge of Portland.

Advances such as the railroad were instrumental in the decline of the Trail.

Ezra Meeker with his oxen and wagon in Kearny, Nebraska, 1906

# EZRA MEEKER

Ezra Meeker settled with his family in Oregon in 1852. In 1906, at the age of 76, he set out in a covered wagon to retrace his journey from west to east. Meeker met with Presidents **Theodore Roosevelt** and **Calvin Coolidge**, stressing the importance of preserving the Oregon Trail. He also testified before Congress. He died in 1928 after making an important effort to protect the Oregon Trail, which is today a national treasure.

Ezra Meeker, a trail pioneer

41

The earth is still rutted from thousands of wagons that headed west.

**Ball, John** (1794-1884) - A member of Nat Wyeth's expedition to Oregon who founded the first American school there.

**Barlow, Samuel K.** (1795-1867) - Oregon pioneer who built a road around Mt. Hood, bypassing the last stretch of the Columbia River.

**Benton, Thomas Hart** (1782-1858) - U.S. Senator from Missouri (1821-1851).

**Bridger, Jim** (1804-1881) - Mountain man who discovered the Great Salt Lake and the area now known as Yellowstone Park.

**Carson, Kit** (1809-1868) - U.S. trapper, guide, and soldier; eventually superintendent of Indian affairs for Colorado territory.

**Clark, William** (1770-1838) - U.S. Army officer who, along with Meriwether Lewis, led the exploration of the Louisiana Purchase (1804-1806).

**Coolidge, Calvin** (1872-1933) - 30th president of the U.S. (1923-1929).

**De Smet, Pierre Jean** (1801-1870) - Belgian Jesuit missionary, founder of many missions in the American West.

**Floyd, John** (1783-1837) - U.S. Congressman from Virginia (1817-1829).

**Frémont, John** (1813-1890) - U.S. explorer and general.

**Gray, Robert** (1755-1806) - U.S. sea captain and explorer who discovered and named the Columbia River (1792).

**Greeley, Horace** (1811-1872) - U.S. journalist who founded the *New York Tribune*, and wrote editorials in the 1850s urging settlers to "Go West, young man, go West."

**Jefferson, Thomas** (1743-1826) - Third president of the U.S. (1801-1809).

**Kelley, Hall Jackson** - (1790-1874) - Massachusetts teacher who planned to lead 3,000 New England farmers to Oregon in the 1830s, not succeeding but inspiring Nathaniel Wyeth.

**Lee, Jason** (1803-1845) - Methodist minister who became the first missionary to Oregon.

**Maxwell, Lucien** (1818-1875) - Fur trader and mountain man who guided John Frémont on the Oregon Trail in 1842.

**McLoughlin, John** - (1784-1857) British head of the Hudson's Bay Company's headquarters at Fort Vancouver from 1825 to 1846.

**O'Sullivan, John L.** (1813-1895) - Editor of the *New York Morning News*, who wrote in 1845 that the U.S. had a "manifest destiny" to occupy the entire North American continent.

**Parker, Samuel** (1779-1866) - Presbyterian missionary to Oregon in 1836.

**Polk, James K.** (1795-1849) - 11th president of the U.S. (1845-1849).

**Roosevelt, Theodore** (1858-1919) - 26th president of the U.S. (1901-1909).

**Smith, Jedediah** (1798-1831) - Mountain man and Indian fighter who guided caravans on the Santa Fe and Oregon trails.

**Smith, Solomon** (1809-1876) - A pioneer with Nat Wyeth's first expedition, who settled in Oregon in 1832.

**Spalding, Eliza** - Wife of Presbyterian missionary Henry Spalding; one of the first two European-American women in Oregon territory.

**Spalding, Henry** (1803-1874) - Presbyterian missionary to Oregon territory in 1836, who established a mission at Lapwai, Idaho, among the Nez Percé.

# KEY PEOPLE *(continued)*

**Stuart, Robert** - Beaver trapper who discovered South Pass in 1812.

**Sublette, William** (1799-1845) - Fur trader and mountain man; built Fort William, which later became Fort Laramie.

**Sutter, John** (1803-1880) - Born Johann Sutter in Switzerland, emigrated to U.S. in 1834, built a fort near Sacramento, California, in 1843. Gold discovered there in 1848 caused the California Gold Rush.

**Tibbetts, Calvin** (1803-1870) - A pioneer with Nathaniel Wyeth's first expedition to Oregon, who settled there in 1832.

**Walker, Joseph** (1798-1876) - Mountain man who led the first wagon train of immigrants into California in 1841.

**Walker, William** (1799-1874) - Wyandot Native who wrote about the 1831 visit to St. Louis, Missouri, of three Nez Percé and one Flathead men, interpreting their visit as a search for religious instruction.

**Whitman, Marcus** (1802-1847) - Presbyterian missionary to Oregon, establishing a mission among the Cayuse at Walla Walla, Washington, in 1836.

**Whitman, Narcissa** (1808-1847) - Wife of Marcus Whitman, one of the first two European-American women in Oregon.

**Wyeth, Nathaniel** (1802-1856) - Boston businessman who assembled the first caravan to travel from St. Louis to Oregon territory in 1832.

---

# A TIMELINE OF THE HISTORY OF
## — THE OREGON TRAIL —

| | |
|---|---|
| **1803** | President Jefferson buys Louisiana Territory for $15 million. |
| **1804-1806** | The Lewis and Clark Expedition explores the new territory, crossing the Rocky Mountains and camping near the mouth of the Columbia River for the winter. |
| **1807-1814** | Journals from the Lewis and Clark Expedition are published. |
| **1820-1840** | Mountain men engaged in fur trapping and trading use Indian paths that later become sections of the Oregon Trail. |

| | |
|---|---|
| **1832** | Nathaniel Wyeth's first expedition to Oregon country. |
| **1834** | Wyeth's second expedition brings the first missionary to Oregon. |
| **1836** | Missionaries Marcus Whitman and Henry Spalding travel with their wives to Oregon, founding missions among the Cayuse and Nez Percé. |
| **1843** | First wagon train on the Oregon Trail. |
| **1843** | The "great migration" of more than 1,000 settlers heads for Oregon. |
| **1840-1860** | More than 300,000 pioneers travel the Oregon Trail. |
| **1844** | James Polk is elected president on an expansionist platform. |
| **1846** | The northern U.S. border with British Canada is established at the 49th parallel. |
| **1847-48** | Brigham Young leads Mormon pioneers to Utah and founds Salt Lake City. |
| **1849** | Seeking gold in California, 25,000 argonauts travel the Oregon Trail. |
| **1862** | Congress passes the Homestead Act, and by 1890 two million people have moved into the West and claimed land as provided by the Act. |
| **1869** | Completion of the transcontinental railroad makes the Oregon Trail obsolete. |
| **1978** | The Oregon Trail is designated a National Historic Trail. |

# GLOSSARY

**acquisition** - Something that is acquired or gained.

**alkaline** - Having a pH (measurement of acidity) higher than 7. Numbers below 7 increase in acidity and numbers above 7 increase in alkalinity.

**argonaut** - An adventurer engaged in a quest, especially one for gold.

**booster** - An enthusiastic supporter.

**California Trail** - Beginning about 1841, an offshoot of the Oregon Trail that began either at Fort Bridger, Wyoming, or Soda Springs, Idaho, and ended near Sacramento, California.

**Catholic** - A member of the universal Christian church.

**Cayuse** - A Native American group of Oregon and Washington.

**census** - A periodic count of a population.

**cholera** - A disease of humans and domestic animals caused by a poison produced by a comma-shaped bacterium.

**clergy** - People ordained to serve as ministers, pastors, or priests in a church.

**continental** - Relating to a continent, especially the part of a country on a specific continent or land mass.

**covered wagon** - A wagon with a canvas top supported by curved strips of wood or metal.

**decade** - A period of 10 years.

**doctrine** - A statement of government policy, especially in international relations.

**economy** - Careful use of resources; the economic structure of a country.

**emigrant** - A person who leaves his or her place of residence or country to live elsewhere.

**epidemic** - Tending to affect a large number of individuals, spreading among them rapidly.

**expansionist** - A person who believes that a nation should expand its territory.

**fertile** - Productive; capable of growing, developing, or reproducing.

**Flathead** - A group of Native Americans in the area of Montana.

**Fort Bridger** - A supply post built by Jim Bridger in 1841-43 east of the Great Salt Lake.

**Fort Hall** - A supply post Nat Wyeth built in 1834 on the Snake River in southern Idaho.

**Fort Laramie** - A trading post originally built in 1835 as Fort William in present-day southeast Wyoming, and later rebuilt as Fort Laramie.

**frontier** - A border between two countries; a region on the edge of developed territory.

**humid** - Containing noticeable moisture; very damp.

**immigrant** - A person who moves into a country from somewhere else.

**impenetrable** - Not able to be pierced.

**inhospitable** - Not friendly or receptive.

**institution** - An established organization or a significant practice.

**Jesuit** - A member of the Roman Catholic Society of Jesus founded in 1534.

**Lewis and Clark Expedition** - Exploration of the Louisiana Purchase and the country beyond, ordered by President Jefferson and carried out from 1804 to 1806 by Meriwether Lewis and William Clark.

**malaria** - A human disease caused by parasites in the red blood cells and spread by the bites of mosquitoes.

**maneuver** - To make changes in direction and position.

**Methodist** - A branch of the Protestant church descended from the Church of England.

**migrant** - A person or animal who moves from place to place.

**migrate** - To move from one country or place to another.

**migration** - Movement from one country or place to another.

**militia** - A body of citizens organized as for military service.

**missionary** - A person undertaking a mission, especially a religious mission.

**Mormon** - Relating to the Church of Jesus Christ of Latter-day Saints.

**mountain man** - An American frontiersman who usually began as a beaver trapper and ended up as an explorer, guide, or settler.

**Nez Percé** - A Native American group of Washington, Idaho, and Oregon.

**Oregon Trail** - Emigrant route to the Northwest, reaching from Independence,

Missouri, to the mouth of the Columbia River.

**parallel** - When referring to latitude, a line running east-west around the globe and measured from the equator to describe a location on the earth.

**perilous** - Full of danger.

**persecution** - The practice of harassing, to the point of injury, people who differ (for example in origin or beliefs) from the people in charge.

**pioneer** - First in anything; one of the first to settle a territory.

**Plains** - Relating to the Native Americans of the Great Plains.

**Plateau** - Relating to Native Americans belonging to more than two dozen tribes who lived on the Columbia Plateau of the Pacific Northwest.

**platform** - Declaration of principles and policies by a group or candidate.

**portage** - The work of carrying or transporting goods, especially overland.

**Preemption Act** - A law Congress passed in 1841 giving first right of land purchase to settlers on unclaimed land.

**Presbyterian** - A branch of the Protestant Church founded in 16th century Scotland.

**prodigious** - Extraordinary in size or quantity; exciting amazement or wonder.

**rationale** - An underlying reason or explanation.

**recession** - A period of reduced economic activity.

**republic** - A government having a chief of state who is not a monarch, but usually a president.

**scarlet fever** - A contagious disease characterized by fever, red rash, and infection of nose, throat, and mouth.

**Shoshone** - A Native American group originally ranging from California through Wyoming and speaking an Uto-Aztecan language.

**Sierra Nevada** - Spanish for "snowy saw-toothed mountains"; a high mountain system in eastern California.

**teem** - To be filled to overflowing; present in large quantity.

**terrain** - The physical features of a tract of land or region.

**territory** - A geographical area; in the United States, an area under its control, with a separate legislature, but not yet a state.

**transcontinental** - Extending across a continent, such as a railway.

**tuberculosis** - A somewhat contagious disease caused by a bacterium and affecting the lungs.

**typhoid** - An infectious disease caused by a bacterium and marked by fever and intestinal inflammation.

**War of 1812** - Conflict between the U.S. and Britain (1812-1815) triggered by the British seizing U.S. sailors to serve on British warships.

**Wyandot** - Refers to a Native American group formed in the 17th century by Hurons and other eastern tribes.

---

**Books of Interest**

Furbee, Mary Rodd. *Outrageous Women of the American Frontier*, John Wiley & Sons, 2002.

Morley, Jacqueline. *You Wouldn't Want to Be an American Pioneer! A Wilderness You'd Rather Not Tame*, Franklin Watts, Inc., 2002.

Thompson, Gare. *Our Journey West: An Adventure on the Oregon Trail*, National Geographic, 2003.

Uschan, Michael V. *The Oregon Trail*, World Almanac, 2004.

Wadsworth, Ginger. *Words West: Voices of Young Pioneers*, Clarion Books, 2003.

**Web Sites**

http://www.americanwest.com/trails/pages/oretrail.htm

http://www.oregontrailcenter.org/

http://www.isu.edu/~trinmich/Oregontrail.html

http://www.pbs.org/weta/thewest/places/trails_ter/oregon.htm

47

# INDEX

---

Linda Thompson is a Montana native and a graduate of the University of Washington. She was a teacher, writer, and editor in the San Francisco Bay Area for 30 years and now lives in Taos, New Mexico. She can be contacted through her web site,

http://www.highmesaproductions.com